CELEBRATING THE NAME JORDAN

Celebrating the Name Jordan

Walter the Educator

Silent King Books

SILENT KING BOOKS

SKB

Copyright © 2024 by Walter the Educator

All rights reserved. No part of this book may be reproduced in any manner whatsoever without written permission except in the case of brief quotations embodied in critical articles and reviews.

First Printing, 2024

Disclaimer
This book is a literary work; the story is not about specific persons, locations, situations, and/or circumstances unless mentioned in a historical context. Any resemblance to real persons, locations, situations, and/or circumstances is coincidental. This book is for entertainment and informational purposes only. The author and publisher offer this information without warranties expressed or implied. No matter the grounds, neither the author nor the publisher will be accountable for any losses, injuries, or other damages caused by the reader's use of this book. The use of this book acknowledges an understanding and acceptance of this disclaimer.

dedicated to everyone with the first name of Jordan

JORDAN

In the ancient groves where the olive trees sway,

Jordan

Jordan's essence echoes in the gentle fray,

Jordan

With roots that delve deep into history's core,

Jordan

A name revered, evermore.

Jordan

Like the river that carves through rugged terrain,

Jordan

Jordan's path is both struggle and gain,

Jordan

Flowing with purpose, steadfast and true,

Jordan

A journey renewed in each morning dew.

Jordan

In the desert where silence holds sway,

Jordan

Jordan brings life in an arid display,

Jordan

A name like an oasis, cool and serene,

Jordan

Where dreams are nurtured in a quiet sheen.

Jordan

In the bustling city, where life is a chase,

Jordan

Jordan strides with an elegant grace,

Jordan

A name that balances the old and the new,

Jordan

With wisdom accrued and insights askew.

Jordan

From the star-studded sky to the ocean's embrace,

Jordan

Jordan's essence touches every place,

Jordan

A name that holds the power to inspire,

Jordan

To kindle hearts with an unyielding fire.

Jordan

Through the cycles of moon and sun,

Jordan

Jordan's journey is never done,

Jordan

A name that embodies the spirit of quest,

Jordan

Seeking the paths that are ever best.

Jordan

In the whispers of the wind through the trees,

Jordan

Jordan finds solace, a moment of ease,

Jordan

A name that is both tranquil and bold,

Jordan

A story that continually unfolds.

Jordan

Across the tapestry of time's vast span,

Jordan

Jordan is more than just a man or woman,

Jordan

A symbol of strength, of hope, and of dreams,

Jordan

Weaving life's fabric with vibrant seams.

Jordan

In the quiet of the night, where stars gently gleam,

Jordan

Jordan ponders life's intricate scheme,

Jordan

A name that holds questions, profound and deep,

Jordan

Guarding secrets that shadows keep.

Jordan

With each sunrise, a promise anew,

Jordan

Jordan embraces the day with a view,

Jordan

A name that dances with the light,

Jordan

Unfurling wings, taking flight.

Jordan

ABOUT THE CREATOR

Walter the Educator is one of the pseudonyms for Walter Anderson. Formally educated in Chemistry, Business, and Education, he is an educator, an author, a diverse entrepreneur, and he is the son of a disabled war veteran. "Walter the Educator" shares his time between educating and creating. He holds interests and owns several creative projects that entertain, enlighten, enhance, and educate, hoping to inspire and motivate you.

> Follow, find new works, and stay up to date
> with Walter the Educator™
> at WaltertheEducator.com

Milton Keynes UK
Ingram Content Group UK Ltd.
UKHW052258300624
444825UK00012B/282